SCIENTIFIC RIVALRIES
AND SCANDALS

DECODING
OUR
DNA

CRAIG VENTER VS THE HUMAN GENOME PROJECT

KAREN GUNNISON BALLEN

Twenty-First Century Books
Minneapolis

In loving memory of Tamara Grace Ballen, 1948–2010

I thank Christine Zuchora-Walske
for her editorial guidance.

Twenty-First Century Books
A division of Lerner Publishing Group, Inc.
241 First Avenue North
Minneapolis, MN 55401 U.S.A.

Website address: www.lernerbooks.com

Library of Congress Cataloging-in-Publication Data

Ballen, Karen Gunnison.
    Decoding our DNA : Craig Venter vs the Human
Genome Project / by Karen Gunnison Ballen.
        p.   cm. — (Scientific rivalries and scandals)
    Includes bibliographical references and index.
    ISBN 978-0-7613-5489-5 (lib. bdg. : alk. paper)
    1. Human gene mapping—Juvenile literature.
    2. Human Genome Project—Juvenile literature. 3. Venter,
J. Craig—Juvenile literature. I. Title.
    QH445.2.B35 2013
    611'.0181663—dc23   2011045644

Manufactured in the United States of America
1 – MG – 7/15/12

CONTENTS

THE CROWN JEWEL OF BIOLOGY

On May 8, 1998, Craig Venter, a talented geneticist, met Francis Collins, the head of the publicly funded Human Genome Project (HGP), at the United Airlines Red Carpet Club at Dulles Airport near Washington, D.C.

Venter had once been part of the HGP, but conflicts with the program's leaders had led him to leave. The company that he'd worked for since had been a thorn in the HGP's side for several years.

To Collins's dismay, Venter explained that he and his colleagues planned to launch a new company that would sequence the human genome faster

Biologist Craig Venter *(left)* and geneticist Francis Collins *(right)* led what became one of the great races of twentieth-century science—to map the human genome. This sequence of thousands of genes determines all human characteristics, from eye color to the risk of certain diseases.

and cheaper than the HGP. Venter proposed that his new company and the HGP would share their data—and presumably the credit—once the job was complete. But plans change.

Scientists, doctors, journalists, and politicians around the world have called the sequencing of the human genome "the crown jewel of twentieth-century biology." Scientists long dreamed of sequencing the human genome. They knew that it would be an enormous task. It would involve figuring out the exact order of the three billion chemical building blocks that make up human DNA. They also knew that the scientists who accomplished this monumental task would win respect and admiration from generations to come. They might also earn money and a place in history.

Why is the human genome so important? The answer to that question lies in the definition of *genome*. An organism's genome is all the deoxyribonucleic

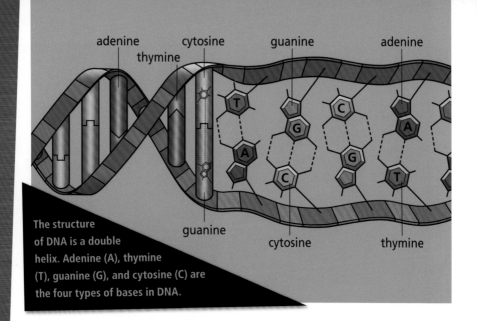

adenine   cytosine   guanine   adenine
thymine

The structure
of DNA is a double
helix. Adenine (A), thymine
(T), guanine (G), and cytosine (C) are
the four types of bases in DNA.

guanine   cytosine   thymine

acid (DNA) in that organism. DNA is a molecule that contains the instructions a cell (the basic unit of all organisms) needs to make proteins, which carry out the chemical processes that maintain life, such as turning food into energy and reproducing. It also determines how the organism looks and behaves. DNA passes from parent to offspring during reproduction. This process is called heredity.

The human genome tells us how we differ from and resemble other organisms. It also tells us how we differ from and resemble one another. It helps us understand how our bodies work—and why they sometimes don't work well. It can guide our efforts to diagnose, treat, and prevent certain diseases.

The Human Genome Project, which launched in 1990, brought together some of the brightest, most creative minds in biology. This group of scientists from around the world worked collaboratively to put together one of science's greatest puzzles. At first, the project was slow. In fact, the original time frame for putting the puzzle together was fifteen years. But some researchers grew impatient with HGP's pace. Businesses recognized this as an opportunity. They saw that a private company could likely beat HGP to the finish line. Then that company could patent the sequence—acquire the exclusive legal right to use or sell it—and make huge profits.

THE RACE IS ON

Craig Venter, a talented researcher involved with HGP's work, was a vocal critic of HGP. He said it was too expensive, disorganized, and inefficient. He believed he could complete the project four years faster and at less cost. So he accepted an offer to become president of a new private genome sequencing company that would compete head-to-head with the HGP.

The race between the two groups soon became a bitter contest. Scientists argued over whether the sequence data should be freely available to the public or privately owned by the scientists who produced it. Cultural differences came into play as well. Europeans generally disapproved of patenting the human genome. They felt strongly that the genome belongs to all humankind. In contrast, many Americans believed that people who worked hard to decode the genome had a right to profit from their efforts. This is the story of how an international scientific collaboration dissolved into a public "mud-wrestling match."

CHAPTER 1

HUMBLE
BEGINNINGS

Long ago, people realized that plants and animals pass traits to their offspring. Farmers used selective breeding (or crossbreeding) to improve their crops and livestock.

They bred animals and plants to encourage reproduction of favorable traits. But no one truly understood how heredity worked.

THE BIRTH OF GENETICS

The field of genetics (the study of heredity) began in the mid-1800s. Gregor Mendel, an Austrian scientist, performed breeding experiments with pea plants to study how the plant passes on certain traits. For example, Mendel bred a plant with round peas and a plant with wrinkled peas. All the offspring had round peas. When Mendel crossed two of the offspring, one-quarter of *their* offspring had wrinkled peas. Mendel concluded that the factors that cause different traits, such as round versus wrinkled peas, occur in paired units. One type of unit is dominant. The other type is recessive. A dominant unit hides a recessive unit with which it is paired. Modern scientists call these units genes, which are segments of DNA that contain instructions for making proteins.

By the late 1800s, microscopes enabled scientists to see structures inside cells. They saw chromosomes—long, coiled strands of DNA—inside cells, though they did not know what chromosomes were. In the early 1900s, scientists studied dividing cells and realized that chromosomes were responsible for heredity. They deduced that chromosomes must contain genes.

Botanist Gregor Mendel set up experiments with pea plants at the Austrian monastery where he and other monks lived in the mid-1800s. He bred the plants to see how various traits would pass from one generation to the next.

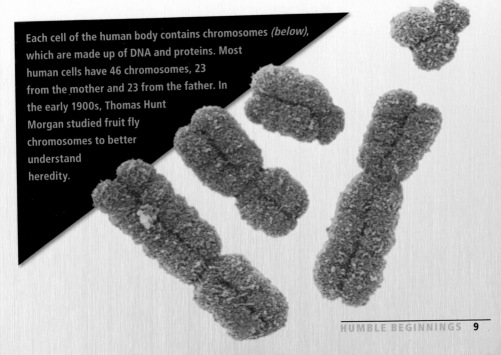

Each cell of the human body contains chromosomes (below), which are made up of DNA and proteins. Most human cells have 46 chromosomes, 23 from the mother and 23 from the father. In the early 1900s, Thomas Hunt Morgan studied fruit fly chromosomes to better understand heredity.

MAPMAKERS

One of these scientists, Thomas Hunt Morgan, went on to study heredity in fruit flies. In 1910 he discovered that the fruit flies' eye color gene was on a specific chromosome called the X chromosome, as were several other genes. But, he noted, fruit flies did not always inherit all of these X-chromosome genes together. Morgan suggested that chromosomes occasionally broke and recombined, meaning that they exchanged segments. He said that genes usually inherited together must be near one another on the same chromosome. Nearness made separation less likely. This idea is called genetic linkage.

Morgan explained his idea to one of his students, Alfred Sturtevant. Sturtevant, intrigued, pored over Morgan's fruit fly records. He wanted to figure out how often each of five genes known to be on the fly's X chromosome was inherited with each of the other genes. Using this information, Sturtevant created the first genetic map. His map was a diagram showing the relative positions of the genes on the X chromosome and the spacing between them.

Morgan called Sturtevant's genetic map "one of the most amazing developments in the whole history of biology." And Morgan was correct. Sturtevant's map was remarkably accurate, and it dramatically improved our understanding of heredity. Sturtevant's map served as the basis for all later genetic maps, including those built by the Human Genome Project in the late 1900s.

Morgan went on to build genetic maps of other fruit fly chromosomes with another student, Calvin Bridges. Morgan and Bridges showed that some traits depend on a combination of many different genes, not just a pair of genes. In addition, Bridges saw that some mutations (sudden, spontaneous changes in the chemical building blocks of genes) changed the appearance of the chromosomes on which the mutations occurred. Bridges used all this information to construct genetic maps. Bridges's maps reflected both the physical and the genetic makeup of chromosomes.

GENES, PROTEINS, AND DNA

By the early 1900s, scientists knew that proteins were responsible for cellular activities. The human body contains thousands of different proteins. Each protein is a long string of molecules called amino acids. The order of amino acids determines what task a protein will perform. For example, structural proteins build or repair parts of the cell. Proteins called enzymes make chemical reactions occur more quickly or at lower temperatures. Without proteins, cells couldn't function.

Scientists suspected that genes and proteins were related somehow. In 1908 English physician Archibald Garrod had found that defective enzymes caused some diseases in humans. Garrod suggested that genes controlled the making of these enzymes.

In 1928 British microbiologist Frederick Griffith showed that living bacteria could pick up traits from dead bacteria. But he did not know what factor enabled the transformation. He suggested that some substance was responsible. This suggestion sparked efforts to identify and describe the substance.

By the early 1940s, scientists knew that ultraviolet (UV) light and X-rays could cause gene mutations. In 1941 geneticist George Beadle and biochemist Edward Tatum exposed a mold to both types of radiation. The exposure changed the enzymes that the mold made. This experiment supported Garrod's 1908 suggestion that genes control enzyme production.

In 1944 biologist Oswald Avery and his colleagues showed that the substance that carried the traits in Griffith's 1928 bacteria experiment was probably DNA. In 1952 geneticists Alfred Hershey and Martha Chase used viruses to prove that DNA is indeed the substance that contains genetic information.

DISCOVERING DNA'S STRUCTURE

By the early 1950s, scientists knew the basic components of DNA. In the late 1800s, German scientist Albrecht Kossel had found that chromosomes were made up of phosphate, a sugar called deoxyribose, and four nucleotide bases: adenine (A), cytosine (C), guanine (G), and thymine (T).

But until the 1950s, scientists didn't know how the components fit together. Nor did they know the complete structure of DNA.

In 1951 Rosalind Franklin, a British chemist, sent X-rays through a DNA molecule to create a photographic image of the molecule. The image showed an X pattern. Scientists knew that this pattern meant the molecule had a helix shape. (A helix is a spiral, like a coiled spring.)

Rosalind Franklin took this X-ray diffraction photo of a DNA molecule in 1953. The X shape told scientists that DNA's structure is a helix.

By studying this image closely and using their knowledge of nucleotide structure, American biologist James Watson and British biologist Francis Crick figured out the structure of DNA in 1953. They realized that a DNA molecule is a double helix. It's shaped like a twisted ladder. The sides of the ladder are chains of deoxyribose and phosphate. The rungs of the ladder are the nucleotide bases, which always occur in pairs. A always binds to T, and C always binds to G.

"They [Watson and Crick] shared the sublime arrogance of men who had never met their intellectual equals."

Max Perutz, colleague of Watson and Crick, 1993

ROSALIND FRANKLIN

Rosalind Franklin was a talented scientist at King's College in London, England, in the early 1950s. At the time, women scientists did not get much respect there. A man who was Franklin's equal treated her as an assistant, and she was not allowed in the commons area used by male scientists.

Franklin used a technique called X-ray crystallography to determine the structure of DNA molecules. One of her coworkers showed Watson a picture Franklin had taken of a DNA molecule without asking her permission. The picture gave Watson the information he and Crick needed to determine the structure of DNA. Franklin's input had been critical to Watson and Crick's accomplishment, but they did not acknowledge her in their article about the structure of DNA.

Franklin went on to publish many articles and to lecture in Europe and North America. She died in 1958.

Rosalind Franklin was a British biophysicist. In the early 1950s, she produced extremely high-quality X-ray images of DNA crystals. Her work was key to the discovery of the double helix structure of DNA.

Along with molecular biologist Maurice Wilkins, James Watson *(left)* and Francis Crick *(right)* won a Nobel Prize in 1962 for their work on confirming the structure of DNA. In this photo from 1953, Watson and Crick pose with their model of a DNA molecule.

DNA must replicate, or make new copies of itself, for cell division to occur. Cell division enables an organism to grow, heal, and reproduce. In 1957 Crick described how DNA replicates. He explained that the molecule "unzips" to form two separate parent strands. Each parent strand serves as a template for a new strand. A complementary base binds to each base on the parent strand according to the rules of base pairing. That is, a T binds to each A, an A to each T, a C to each G, and a G to each C. Crick compared DNA replication with a hand in a glove. When the hand and glove come apart, each can serve as a mold for a new partner.

In 1958 Crick described how DNA directs protein synthesis (the making of proteins). First, the DNA unzips. Then DNA transcription occurs. Each parent strand serves as a template for a molecule of messenger ribonucleic acid (mRNA). An RNA molecule is similar to a DNA molecule, but RNA has just one sugar-phosphate strand. And RNA's four nucleotide bases are A, C, G, and U (uracil instead of thymine). The next step of protein synthesis is called translation. In this step, the mRNA travels to the ribosomes (tiny structures inside cells that assemble proteins). The ribosomes "read" the mRNA and use its code, or pattern of nucleotide bases, to identify specific amino acids called for by the code. Other structures in the cell bring the appropriate amino acids, which join to form a specific protein.

The instructions in DNA and RNA are called the genetic code. The code is made up of codons. Each codon contains three nucleotide bases. Each codon either specifies an amino acid or starts or stops translation. The order of codons in a segment of DNA determines the order of amino acids in a protein.

A mutation in DNA changes the order of nucleotides within a codon. If the mutated codon produces the same amino acid as the original codon, the mutation is harmless. If the mutated codon produces a different amino acid than the original codon, it might change the final structure of the protein. Changes in structure change a protein's function. Some altered proteins do not function at all.

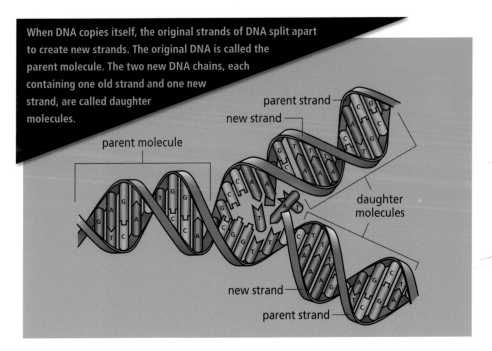

When DNA copies itself, the original strands of DNA split apart to create new strands. The original DNA is called the parent molecule. The two new DNA chains, each containing one old strand and one new strand, are called daughter molecules.

parent strand
new strand
parent molecule
daughter molecules
new strand
parent strand

TOOLS OF THE TRADE

DNA molecules are very long. To work with DNA, scientists needed a way to break the long strands into shorter pieces. In the 1960s, several scientists discovered that bacteria make special enzymes to protect themselves against viruses. These enzymes, called restriction enzymes, cut viral DNA molecules into smaller pieces. In 1970 American microbiologist Hamilton Smith found that a bacterium called *Haemophilus influenzae* makes a restriction enzyme that cuts DNA only at specific sites—that is, only where it recognizes specific sequences of nucleotide bases. Since then, scientists have identified restriction enzymes that cut DNA at more than 150 different sites.

In the 1970s, British biochemist Fred Sanger developed a method of sequencing DNA, or finding the order of nucleotide bases on a stretch of DNA. Sanger knew that when DNA replicates inside a cell, the DNA first unzips into two strands. Then an enzyme called DNA polymerase builds new complementary strands of DNA using the old strands as templates. For example, at each A in the template, the enzyme inserts a T in the new strand. Sanger made a mixture of DNA templates, DNA polymerase, and nucleotide bases. In this mixture, the polymerase built new strands of DNA based on the templates.

Next, Sanger made four different mixtures. Each mixture included DNA templates, DNA polymerase, regular nucleotide bases, and a special form of one of the four bases that could bind to the end of a growing strand but could not bind to a new base. The special bases are called terminal bases because they stop a DNA strand from growing any longer. This time, strand building stopped anytime the polymerase inserted a terminal base into a growing DNA strand. This process formed many new DNA strands of different lengths. The shortest strands had just one base (which paired with the first base on the template). The second-shortest strands had two bases (which paired with the first two bases on the template), and so on until the longest strands had as many bases as the template strand.

To separate the strands of different sizes, Sanger used a method called gel electrophoresis. This gel is a rectangular slab that feels like stiff gelatin and has wells near one end. Sanger loaded his mixtures of DNA fragments of different lengths into the wells so that each well contained a mixture with a different type of terminal base (A, C, G, or T). He applied an electrical current to the gel. The current made the DNA fragments move through the gel. DNA fragments of the same length traveled together in a group. The smaller fragments moved faster. For this reason, the groups of DNA fragments spread out through the gel according to their sizes. Each group formed a band in the gel. Sanger used a special type of photography that made the bands show up in a picture. By looking at the picture, moving from the bottom (shortest strand) to the top, Sanger could "read" the sequence of the DNA strand.

GENOME SEQUENCING BEGINS

Sanger quickly put his sequencing technique to work. In 1977 his team completed the first DNA genome sequence. The genome belonged to a virus called phi X174. The genome was relatively small. It contained just 5,386 nucleotides. Sanger's team had spent more than two years sequencing it.

In the early 1980s, Americans Michael Hunkapiller and Leroy Hood improved Sanger's sequencing technique by automating it. They developed a method of labeling the terminal bases with different-colored dyes. With this new labeling method, a computer could identify the bases to determine their sequence.

Also, a new, faster technique replaced gel electrophoresis. So scientists could sequence DNA at least ten times faster than before. Automation and speed allowed DNA sequencing to happen on a much larger scale.

CHAPTER 2

THE HUMAN

GENOME

During the 1900s, scientists made many leaps in understanding and analyzing DNA. They figured out DNA's structure and function. They also came up with the first methods for sequencing DNA.

These advances made new leaps possible. For example, in the early 1980s, scientists learned to identify markers on the human genome. Markers are DNA sequences whose inheritance pattern can be followed. Researchers studied the DNA of people in families with genetic diseases. They identified markers for some of those diseases. The markers were DNA sequences located near the disease-causing gene but not within the gene. Using these markers, researchers could identify the approximate locations of many disease genes on the human genome.

In May 1985, Robert Sinsheimer, biologist and chancellor of the University of California–Santa Cruz, organized a meeting of many well-known geneticists. They discussed the possibility of a huge research project: sequencing the human genome. Then, in 1986, Italian scientist Renato Dulbecco published an influential article in the journal *Science*. In this article, Dulbecco independently suggested that scientists sequence the human genome. He emphasized that this accomplishment could aid the fight against cancer.

Italian-born virologist (scientist who studies viruses) Renato Dulbecco won a Nobel Prize in 1975 for his study of cancer-causing viruses. Dulbecco was among many scientists who suggested the international effort to sequence the human genome.

He encouraged scientists to collaborate internationally. Meanwhile, the U.S. Department of Energy (DOE) Office of Health and Environmental Research (OHER) was studying the effects of radiation on the human genome. OHER wanted to compare the genomes of survivors of nuclear bombing to a model human genome. From these sources, the Human Genome Project was born.

SKEPTICISM

But many scientists wondered whether sequencing the human genome was worthwhile. The task would be very expensive—an estimated $3 billion. Committing that much money to the HGP meant less funding for other worthwhile projects. And why spend so much money and time sequencing the whole genome? Most of the human genome is noncoding DNA, or DNA that does not code for proteins. Many scientists thought it would be useless to sequence

"The sequence of the human DNA is the reality of our species, and everything that happens in the world depends on those sequences."

Renato Dulbecco, 1986

DISEASE GENES

Generally speaking, genetic diseases arise from mutated genes. When geneticists announce that they've "found the gene for" a particular disease, they mean that they've located the position of a gene whose mutated form causes the disease.

For example, all humans have a gene on chromosome 7 called the CFTR gene. This gene codes for a protein that helps water move into and out of cells. In some people, the CFTR gene is mutated, so it encodes a dysfunctional protein. As a result, water movement is impaired, and cells lining the passages of various organs produce thick mucus that blocks airways and glands. This condition is called cystic fibrosis.

the noncoding DNA. And other researchers argued that they could find genes one by one in the course of research already under way rather than spending new money on the HGP.

Furthermore, many scientists felt that sequencing the full human genome was an impossible task. The technology was still too slow. At the time, scientists had not even succeeded in sequencing the genome of a simple bacterium—roughly three million base pairs. The human genome has three *billion* base pairs organized on twenty-three pairs of chromosomes. In the mid-1980s, scientists thought that the human genome contained one hundred thousand genes. (Modern scientists know that this number is much smaller. According to the latest findings, the human genome has about twenty-five thousand genes.)

The human genome would be much more difficult to analyze than a bacterial genome. The human genome contains hundreds of thousands of sequences of repetitive DNA—sequences in which, for example, "ATATAT" or "GCGCGC" repeats for hundreds of base pairs. Other types of repetitive DNA are hundreds of thousands of base pairs in length. The size and complexity of the human genome made its sequencing a daunting task.

AN INTERNATIONAL EFFORT

In 1989 the National Institutes of Health (NIH) established the National Center for Human Genome Research (NCHGR) as the U.S. arm of the HGP. James Wyngaarden was head of the NIH at the time. Wyngaarden appointed James Watson to lead the NCHGR. Watson was one of the most famous living geneticists. In addition to codiscovering DNA structure as a young man, he'd played a major role in establishing the academic field of molecular biology (the study of molecules in living things). He was also president of the world-famous Cold Spring Harbor Laboratory for biological sciences on Long Island, New York.

Watson had many abilities that qualified him to head the U.S. arm of the HGP. His fame could attract other talented scientists. His leadership skills could encourage people to work together and could build political support. Political support was vital for winning sufficient public funds. And Watson had a clear vision for the project. He insisted that human genome sequencing must be a multinational effort. "It wouldn't be good if the Americans owned the genome," he later explained. Thanks to his efforts, the HGP included large labs in the United States and in the United Kingdom (UK) as well as smaller labs in France, Germany, China, and Japan.

The Sanger Centre in Cambridge became the headquarters of the UK arm of the HGP. At the beginning of the project, the Sanger Centre was the largest sequencing facility in the world. It was funded by the Wellcome Trust, the world's largest private medical charity, and by the Medical Research Council, a UK

> "It wouldn't be good if the Americans owned the genome."
>
> James Watson, 2000

governmental agency. John Sulston was the first director of the Sanger Centre.

The HGP admitted that having many labs around the world working on the same project made it more expensive and harder to manage. But the HGP argued that "the human genome sequence is the common heritage of all humanity and the work should transcend national boundaries."

A METHODICAL APPROACH

The HGP officially began its work in 1990. By this time, scientists had started sequencing the genomes of bacteria, yeast, and small animals. Sequencing these genomes would help scientists improve their techniques, which would, in turn, increase speed and reduce costs. It would also help scientists test the functions of genes in simple organisms. Many different organisms have similar genes, so scientists could apply what they learned from them to the human genome. The HGP's sequencing of several nonhuman genomes won it support from many scientists.

All the sequences that had been discovered were organized on public databases. The U.S. database, established in 1982, was called GenBank. Researchers "deposited" DNA sequences in GenBank, where other researchers could access them easily at no charge. This system of data sharing helped scientists build on one another's work and sped up progress.

Scientists in England were heavily involved in the race to sequence the human genome. They worked from the Sanger Centre *(below)* in Cambridge, which was the UK headquarters of the Human Genome Project.

The HGP planned to sequence the human genome carefully and methodically. The human genome had to be sequenced in small parts and then assembled into whole chromosomes. Most researchers believed that large amounts of repetitive DNA would make assembling the final sequence hard. So the HGP began by making maps showing the locations of known genes on the various human chromosomes—just as Thomas Hunt Morgan and his students had done for fruit flies decades earlier. Others argued that the mapping step was unnecessary and would slow the process.

The HGP intended to use a process called clone-based sequencing to map the human genome. Sequencing machines could read only about five hundred bases at a time. The human genome contains billions of bases, so scientists could not sequence the whole genome at once. Using restriction enzymes, scientists cut human chromosomes into fragments that were between one hundred thousand and two hundred thousand base pairs long. Copies of each chromosome were cut with different restriction enzymes (each of which cut at different sequences) so the final collection of DNA segments would overlap one another. Then the scientists combined each fragment of human DNA with bacterial DNA that had been cut with the same restriction enzyme to form a bacterial artificial chromosome (BAC). The bacterium multiplied many times to form a large number of bacteria, and each new bacterium contained a copy of the BAC. Each batch of bacteria containing the same human DNA fragment is called a clone. Scientists took DNA from each BAC clone, cut it into smaller fragments with a restriction enzyme, and separated the fragments using electrophoresis. The lengths of DNA fragments for each BAC were measured and recorded as that BAC's "fingerprint."

Scientists fingerprinted many different BACs in this way. Then they had to figure out how the fragments fit together to make up the chromosomes. They realized that clones that had been prepared with different restriction enzymes and shared some DNA fragments of similar size were likely to be right next to one another on a chromosome, so that their sequences overlapped. They called these clones overlapping clones. Scientists used the overlaps to arrange the clones in the right order on a map of the chromosome they came from.

DNA Engine Tetrad

In DNA sequencing, DNA is first placed in a bacterial solution *(top left)*. Chemically treated fragments of DNA are then put into a thermal cycler for fluorescent tagging *(top right)*, which a DNA sequencer reads *(bottom left)*. Finally, a computer image *(bottom right)* of sequenced base pairs is generated for scientists to study.

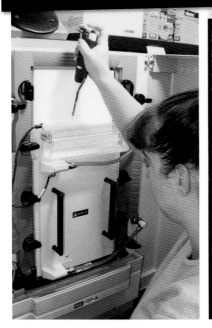
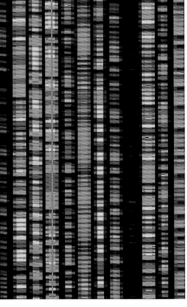

Once the mapping of human chromosomes was complete, sequencing would begin. Scientists would start by sequencing clones. Then they would assemble the BAC sequences into chromosome sequences based on the maps the scientists had already produced. The HGP's approach was careful and methodical, designed to produce a very accurate picture of the human genome. HGP leaders said that the final genome sequence would be 99.99 percent accurate. That meant it would contain only about one error per ten thousand nucleotide bases. Watson made it clear that the HGP's primary goal was to produce a tool for geneticists. The HGP would not focus on disease genes or even on gene-rich portions of the genome. It would sequence the entire genome fragment by fragment and then assemble the complete sequence so that geneticists could work with the data however they liked. This approach ensured accuracy, but it was slow. Some people were losing patience with the HGP.

PRESSURE
FOR PROGRESS

Critics attacked the HGP's slow, methodical, decentralized approach. Medical researchers were eager to locate and analyze genes associated with diseases. They said that they could make lifesaving medical advancements earlier if the HGP used a faster sequencing method. Steven McKnight, cofounder of a biotechnology company, said of the HGP, "It's just a disaster. There is no cohesion, no focus, no game plan. To me, it's typical government work." Another critic complained that the program was run more by politics than by the needs of science. In politics, changing decisions is a sign of weakness. The HGP was rigidly sticking with its plan instead of using improvements in sequencing methods to make faster progress.

CHAPTER 3

THE PATENT
DEBATES

People who knew Craig Venter in his youth probably wouldn't have guessed that he would one day become a brilliant scientist. He was a wild child who did poorly in school.

As a young man, he had a difficult relationship with his father. In the late 1960s, Venter was drafted into the U.S. Navy during the Vietnam War (1959–1975), against which he had protested. He served as a medic in Da Nang, Vietnam. His experiences there inspired him to study medicine. Once he committed himself to study, he did extremely well, receiving a bachelor's degree in biochemistry and a PhD in physiology and pharmacology in only six years.

Venter went on to run a large, productive DNA sequencing lab at the National Institutes of Health. He was eager to speed up the HGP. So he requested an NIH grant for funding to sequence parts of the human X

> "It is impossible to jump-start anything in a field that is so bogged down in laboratory politics that science and data come in a poor second to personality, pride, and ego."
>
> *Craig Venter, 2007*

chromosome. But the review process was very slow. Venter lost patience and withdrew his application. In April 1991, he wrote a letter to James Watson expressing his frustration: "I am concerned that the bureaucracy that is a necessary part of the grant review process cannot keep pace with the rapid developments in the genome area."

EXPRESSED SEQUENCE TAGS

Venter began developing a plan to identify protein-coding regions of chromosomes. This strategy could dramatically speed up the process of gene mapping. To find protein-coding regions, Venter first obtained messenger RNA from human brain tissue. Since noncoding DNA is not transcribed to mRNA, it was not included in these samples. Then Venter used an enzyme called reverse transcriptase to make DNA from the mRNA. He sequenced the first 150 to 400 bases of each strand of DNA. He chose this range because GenBank required sequences to be at least 150 bases in length and because he found that more sequencing mistakes were made beyond 400 bases. These partial gene sequences were called expressed sequence tags, or ESTs, because they included DNA that was "expressed"— transcribed to RNA.

In 1991 Venter reported obtaining more than 600 ESTs from human brain tissue. Of these, 337 genes were new discoveries, so they could be submitted to GenBank. At this time, GenBank contained less than 3,000 human genes. Venter's work was impressive. He had added more than 10 percent more genes to public knowledge in a very short time.

In June 1991, Venter's group published an article in *Science* explaining their EST results. They suggested that their technique could find genes much faster and more cheaply than the HGP's technique could. Venter suggested that the EST method could locate almost as many genes—80 to 90 percent—in the human genome as could the HGP. And it would cost twelve to fifteen cents per base. (The HGP's budget called for one dollar per base sequenced.)

These comments angered many members of the HGP. They felt that Venter was acting out of self-interest, pushing to replace their sequencing method with his. They argued that Venter could not find as many genes as he claimed he could find. They believed he could only find ESTs of genes that were expressed in the tissue he was sampling at the time he sampled it. Some genes are only expressed in some types of tissue—such as muscle or brain tissue. And some genes are only expressed during certain times of our lives—such as when we are children or when we are adults—or even during certain times of the day.

The HGP underscored the importance of noncoding DNA. Some sequences of noncoding DNA determine which genes are expressed and when they are expressed. ESTs do not include these critical genome sequences because they are not transcribed to mRNA. Venter countered that he did not consider the EST strategy as a replacement for the HGP's sequencing effort. Instead, he felt that his strategy could complement the HGP's work. But the HGP didn't want this kind of help. Tensions were beginning to rise.

THE PATENT DEBATES BEGIN

Venter's EST work was clearly valuable to science. So Reid Adler, head of the NIH Office of Technology Transfer, filed a patent application on 347 ESTs found by Venter's lab. Adler explained that he did so to protect American companies. If the NIH held patents on these ESTs, it could transfer the patents to American companies. Those companies could then receive profits from their work in developing products based on the ESTs. Without patent protection, Adler feared, companies would not be willing to spend the money to develop products based on the new technology.

But in 1991, there were no clear rules regarding the patenting of genetic material. Patents had been issued for disease-causing genes after the genes were identified. But ESTs are only partial gene sequences. They aren't actually genes. Nor do they tell anything about a gene's function. The patent application for the ESTs claimed exclusive rights not only to the ESTs but also to the genes they represented and the proteins those genes encoded. Many members of the HGP felt that these claims went much too far.

> "A patent should not be granted for something that is part of our universal heritage."
>
> Hubert Curien, France's minister of research, 1992

HGP's director, James Watson, argued that producing ESTs did not require a new technique, as a patent would indicate. He said that "virtually any monkey" could reproduce Venter's work and that "what is important is interpreting the sequence." Watson's words offended Venter's team, widening the rift between it and the HGP.

In addition, Watson feared that EST patents would undermine the HGP's collaborative spirit. He was not alone. Many HGP leaders thought the NIH's patent claims would spark a patent race among scientists who were supposed to be cooperating. Bernadine Healy, the NIH's new director, defended its EST patent application, arguing that NIH must protect the interests of U.S. companies. She said that the heated discussion about patenting was silly and that it had become a moral-ethical issue instead of an academic one. Healy said that the patent office should determine whether the ESTs were patentable. In 1992 the U.S. Patent Office rejected the first patent application. NIH appealed the rejection and filed new applications on more than four thousand additional ESTs.

Over time, Watson and Healy argued more—and more publicly—over a number of issues. One key point of contention was that Watson held stock in biotech and pharmaceutical companies that did business with the NIH. Because of this, Watson was not allowed to participate in decisions the NIH made regarding funding for those companies. But he had done so. (Watson said that he had not done it intentionally.) According to Watson, Healy used this accusation to put pressure on him to resign from the HGP. But Watson insisted that her real reason for wanting him to resign was because he opposed her desire to seek patents on ESTs. Healy denied this accusation. Watson, who was critical of Venter's research, was further angered when Healy asked Venter to head a committee that would map the future of the NIH's human genome research. By spring the tensions and disagreements between Healy and Watson had mounted dramatically. Watson resigned from the HGP in April 1992, growling, "I don't know anyone who would want to live with my boss."

> "The rationale is not to make money, but rather to promote and encourage the development and commercialization of products to benefit the public and to do so in a socially responsible way."
>
> —Bernadine Healy, 1992

Shortly thereafter, Watson's fears of a patent race came true. In July 1992, the Medical Research Council filed patent applications on twelve hundred partial gene sequences.

VENTER LEAVES THE NIH

By this time, Venter had a lot more ideas for sequencing the human genome that he was eager to try. He had requested money to support his EST research. The NIH denied his request, claiming that ESTs were not useful enough in the quest to sequence the human genome.

But biotechnology companies had begun noticing Venter's work. A biotech entrepreneur named Wallace Steinberg made Venter an appealing offer. Steinberg wanted to set up a nonprofit research center, and he wanted Venter to lead it. The Institute for Genomic Research (TIGR, pronounced "tiger") would be located in Rockville, Maryland. At TIGR Venter could continue generating human ESTs. His team would have state-of-the-art DNA sequencing machines, a supercomputer, and many computer workstations. Steinberg offered Venter a whopping $70 million to fund his work at TIGR.

But under Steinberg's plan, TIGR's EST data would not be freely available to other researchers through GenBank. Instead, Steinberg created a for-profit system. He established a sister company for TIGR called Human Genome Sciences (HGS) and appointed biophysicist William Haseltine to lead HGS. TIGR would give HGS its sequence data, and HGS would apply for patents. This would allow HGS to charge other businesses a fee for the data.

Steinberg's offer was so appealing to Venter that he left NIH in 1992, taking several staff members with him. In addition to funding Venter's work, Steinberg also gave Venter 10 percent of HGS—a share worth $13.4 million. Venter became rich and famous overnight.

Other scientists bitterly resented Venter's success. They felt that he had never invented anything new and useful and was getting attention simply for using existing techniques and machines on a large scale. Some called him Darth Venter, after the evil villain of *Star Wars*. Others pronounced the name of his new company Tigger, after the silly, puffed-up Winnie-the-Pooh character.

John Sulston of the Sanger Centre observed that through TIGR and HGS,

PATENTS

Patents enable inventors to make money for their efforts. A patent holder can charge any price for use of the invention. For example, if HGS patented thousands of ESTs, it could charge exorbitant fees to companies who used the gene sequences to develop treatments. These expenses would lead to high prices on drugs and other treatments for genetic diseases. Researchers who couldn't afford the fees couldn't participate in developing treatments. Furthermore, many people—especially European scientists—felt the human genome belonged to all humans. They believed patenting it was unethical. The issue still plagues scientific research.

Venter could conduct high-powered research, gain academic recognition, and receive a handsome financial reward for his work. Many scientists look down on those who work for financial gain. Venter denied that he was interested in financial gain—but he did jokingly tell a reporter that he took the job at TIGR so he could buy a bigger boat.

SUCCESSES AND STRUGGLES

At TIGR Venter continued building his EST database, producing sequence data at an unprecedented scale. He soon demonstrated the potential of ESTs. In December 1993, cancer researcher Bert Vogelstein contacted Venter. Vogelstein had observed that patients who had a certain type of colon cancer often had mutations on certain chromosomes. He knew that one of these mutations was in a DNA repair gene. A DNA repair gene encodes an enzyme that repairs DNA mutations that might lead to cancer. A mutated DNA repair gene encodes a faulty enzyme that can't repair cancer-causing DNA mutations. Vogelstein thought there must be a mutation in at least one more repair gene.

Vogelstein asked Venter to search TIGR's database for repair genes. Vogelstein provided sequences from yeast and bacterial genes to aid the search. (Different types of organisms have similar genes that code for similar proteins, so researchers expected the human genes to have sequences similar to those of yeast and bacteria.) TIGR found sequences of three repair genes in its database and used them to prepare DNA sequences. TIGR researchers attached fluorescent dyes to the DNA sequences and used them to probe human chromosomes that had been treated to make their strands separate. A probe would bind to a chromosome where it encountered a complementary sequence—a sequence of DNA that had bases complementing those in the probe (according to the rules of base pairing). The probes attached to the chromosome areas where Vogelstein had observed abnormalities in cancer patients.

This was a significant breakthrough. With the exact locations of the genes identified, researchers sequenced repair genes from cancer patients to confirm that mutations in these genes were associated with cancer.

They were. Eventually the link between mutation and disease led to the development of potentially lifesaving diagnostic tests for this type of colon cancer. And the EST strategy proved useful in locating genes for other diseases, such as Alzheimer's.

With these dramatic breakthroughs, leadership at HGS realized they could make huge amounts of money. So Haseltine decided to sell pharmaceutical companies access to TIGR's EST data. SmithKline Beecham, a British pharmaceutical company, paid HGS $125 million for exclusive commercial rights to TIGR's data. SmithKline Beecham also purchased 7 percent of HGS, which enabled it to share in HGS's future profits.

Venter was excited about his work and wanted to publish his research in scientific journals. Yet working for a for-profit company had drawbacks for Venter. Haseltine opposed the publication idea, because HGS and SmithKline Beecham could make more money if TIGR's data stayed private. This inability to share data made Venter even more unpopular with his former colleagues at the NIH.

PUBLIC VS PRIVATE

A private company such as TIGR is very different from a public institution such as the NIH. Venter explained that one feature that attracted him to a private company was less job security—only the best, most motivated scientists could thrive there. But a private company is a risky venture. Scientists have to perform well and make discoveries or inventions that can be used for profit by their employer. They have less freedom to research ideas. And while sharing data is normal for scientists in publicly funded institutions, private companies have strict rules about keeping their information secret to increase their chances of being the first company to develop a new invention.

CHAPTER 4

GENOME
SEQUENCING

After James Watson resigned from the HGP, NIH director Bernadine Healy invited geneticist and physician Francis Collins to replace him.

Collins and his colleagues had identified the gene for cystic fibrosis, the gene for neurofibromatosis (a nerve tumor syndrome), and the gene for Huntington's disease (a disorder that causes dementia and severe muscle problems). He'd also participated in the search for a breast cancer gene. Collins had a strong background in genetics, and other scientists respected him as both an administrator and a communicator.

In addition, Collins had practiced medicine. Watson had emphasized the goal of producing tools for geneticists. Collins, by contrast, emphasized the medical contributions the HGP could make.

Soon after U.S. president Bill Clinton took office in 1993, he appointed Harold Varmus to replace Bernadine Healy as NIH's director. (A new presidential administration often appoints a new NIH director.) Varmus had a long history of promoting open communication among scientists. He quickly withdrew the NIH's EST patent applications, declaring that such patents did not serve the best interests of science or the public. The Medical Research Council followed suit and withdrew its own EST patent applications.

THWARTING THE TIGR–HGS PATENTS

Meanwhile, TIGR kept churning out ESTs, and its sister company HGS kept trying to patent them. In October 1994, Michael Morgan of Wellcome Trust called a meeting of HGP leaders. Morgan asked them to discuss using TIGR's EST collection for mapping human genes.

Collins opposed this idea. He supported a different strategy instead. Merck and other large pharmaceutical companies feared that HGS would succeed at patenting its large collection of ESTs. If that happened, SmithKline Beecham would have exclusive access to the ESTs, from which would come enormous profits. To undercut its competitor and to ensure equal access to the ESTs, Merck provided a large grant to two researchers at Washington University in Saint Louis, Missouri, to quickly produce hundreds of thousands of ESTs. The researchers would make the ESTs available to the public immediately, at no charge. Data in the public domain could not be patented. Other sequencing centers around the

"We have committed more than $100 million to Craig Venter's work at TIGR, as well as an extra $0.5 million in making the database available to the academic community, and feel that we have a reasonable right to profit from any results that emerge from something that we have made an investment in."

George Poste, research director at SmithKline Beecham, 1994

world joined in this effort. In the end, the centers generated a tremendous number of ESTs, and patents were never issued.

THE GENOME DIRECTORY

Venter wanted to increase access to TIGR's data. According to Venter, he convinced his bosses to relax their strict rules so he could make the EST data more public. In 1994 Venter began negotiating with the scientific journal *Nature*. Venter wanted the journal to publish, in a special issue, TIGR's huge collection of EST data as well as that found by the Washington University scientists and other sequencing centers. A special issue of *Nature* devoted to Venter's work would be quite a feather in his cap.

But some geneticists hated the idea, presumably because it would give Venter a great deal of prestige. In fact, one of the leading geneticists in the

SCIENCE AND NATURE

Scientists usually communicate their findings by publishing their work in scientific journals. Scientists read about and discuss one another's work. They learn from and argue with one another.

Science and *Nature* are two prestigious scientific journals. Researchers in a wide variety of fields read both, and the competition among scientists for publication in these journals is fierce. Both journals have published many landmark articles describing world-changing discoveries. (For example, Watson and Crick published their description of DNA structure in a 1953 issue of *Nature*.) *Science* and *Nature* were important vehicles for sharing the findings of scientists working to sequence genomes.

United States threatened *Nature* editor John Maddox. This scientist told Maddox that if *Nature* published the collection, U.S. geneticists would stop submitting their articles to *Nature* altogether, leaving the prestigious journal without access to information on important scientific developments.

Maddox stood his ground.

> "If you publish this Venter stuff, I can promise you that nobody in the US genome community will ever send you anything ever again!"
>
> U.S. geneticist (name withheld), in telephone call to John Maddox, editor of *Nature*, 1995

Nature published "The Genome Directory" in September 1995. It showed that in less than two years, TIGR had made stunning progress. It had doubled the total amount of DNA sequenced by the rest of the world.

WHOLE GENOME SHOTGUN SEQUENCING

In 1994 Venter and Hamilton Smith, the microbiologist who had discovered restriction enzymes, requested NIH funding to sequence the genome of the *Haemophilus influenzae* bacterium. They planned to use a technique called whole genome shotgun sequencing.

In shotgun sequencing, scientists shred all an organism's DNA using a mechanical method, such as ultrasonic waves. They shred the DNA into thousands of random pieces rather than cutting it in predictable locations with restriction enzymes. (The term *shotgun* refers to this random method of breaking up DNA molecules.) Researchers then sequence each piece of DNA, and a computer program identifies overlapping fragments and genetic markers to reassemble the complete genome. Because the process uses no mapping, it requires especially powerful computer programs to locate fragments of DNA that overlap one another on the genome.

The NIH denied Venter and Smith's request for funding. Most scientists believed that because this sequencing method didn't map genes first, the reassembly would be full of errors. But Venter and Smith soon proved them wrong.

In 1995 TIGR announced that it had sequenced the genomes of not one but two species of bacteria using the whole genome shotgun method. First, TIGR published the genome of *Haemophilus influenzae*. At 1.8 million bases, this was the largest genome sequenced to date. Also, this was the first time scientists had sequenced the entire genome of an organism capable of living independently. (Viruses, by contrast, cannot grow and multiply outside a host organism.) Next, Venter and his colleagues published the genome of a second bacterium, *Mycoplasma genitalium*.

TIGR had sequenced two genomes in just one year—lightning fast compared to earlier genome sequencing projects. And TIGR had done so using a technique many geneticists had considered useless. TIGR had sequenced the genomes of the two species several times over—as scientists always do in genome sequencing. This is why the scientists were confident

CLONE-BASED VS SHOTGUN SEQUENCING

One HGP researcher contrasted the clone-based versus whole genome shotgun sequencing processes with an analogy. He compared the human genome to a volume of an encyclopedia. In clone-based sequencing, one takes a single page out of the book, tears it up, and then tries to reassemble it. But the researcher knows all the pieces are part of that page. In whole genome shotgun sequencing, one takes all the pages at once, tears them all up, and tries to reassemble the entire book, with no idea to which page each piece belongs.

that TIGR's sequences were accurate. As a result, whole genome shotgun sequencing became the standard method for sequencing bacterial genomes.

In early 1996, an international coalition of 633 scientists accomplished another huge goal. They sequenced a yeast genome.

Yeasts are single-celled organisms, like bacteria. But yeasts are fungi, which are much more complex than bacteria. Yeast cells are more similar to plant and animal cells in structure and function.

Yeast is an important model organism. Scientists have studied it to learn how the life cycle of a cell is controlled, which is helpful in understanding some diseases.

THE BERMUDA ACCORD

By this time, the HGP was under pressure to make progress more quickly. The Wellcome Trust sponsored an international meeting of HGP leaders in Bermuda. The meeting would improve organization and establish ground rules for the HGP to increase its efficiency.

This meeting produced an agreement called the Bermuda Accord. The document stated that HGP scientists would release all their sequence data into public databases within twenty-four hours of assembly so that others could build on that data. Sharing data would promote speed, efficiency, and cooperation. It would also prevent patenting. This policy affirmed the idea that the human genome belongs to all people.

All the world's major sequencing centers agreed to follow this policy. But in time, its terms would become a source of heated debate.

> "All human genome sequence information should be freely available and in the public domain in order to encourage research and development and to maximize its benefit to society."
>
> Bermuda Accord, 1998

CHAPTER 5

THE GENOME
WAR

TIGR's use of the whole genome shotgun sequencing method on bacteria impressed many scientists. Some suggested using it on the human genome. NIH scientists argued that the results would be full of errors.

Meanwhile, the HGP worked toward another milestone. In 1998 John Sulston of the Sanger Centre and Robert Waterston at Washington University finished sequencing the genome of a roundworm called *Caenorhabditis elegans*—the project's first completed animal genome.

A roundworm, unlike a yeast, is multicellular. So its genome revealed new information about biological processes. Scientists have studied it to learn how different parts of an animal's body interact. This study has helped researchers better understand genes that control traits such as longevity, social interaction, Alzheimer's disease, and cancer.

Even with this important achievement, the HGP had sequenced only 3 percent of the human genome since 1990. And it had already spent about $1.8 billion. It didn't incorporate new ideas and discoveries as they developed. Medical researchers fighting genetic diseases were frustrated with the slow pace of HGP data generation. Many people criticized the HGP's inefficiency, slow progress, and politics. Venter called HGP leaders the "Liar's Club," claiming that they gave completely different answers when asked how much they'd spent and accomplished.

A PRIVATE SEQUENCING COMPANY

By 1998 biochemist Michael Hunkapiller was president of a company that made a highly advanced DNA sequencer. Hunkapiller believed that with

Venter sits near a DNA sequencer in a sequencing lab. By the twenty-first century, sequencers are available in many different sizes and can sequence massive amounts of information rapidly.

hundreds of these new devices, a private company could sequence the entire human genome faster than the HGP could. But Hunkapiller needed someone with vast experience to lead such a company. He courted Venter.

In this company, Venter would have three hundred of Hunkapiller's machines at his disposal. And he'd have one of the world's fastest computers to reassemble the sequenced DNA fragments into a complete genome. The new company would have greater capacity than all the world's other sequencing centers combined. It would also have great prestige. Venter admitted that the "lure of the genome" was strong.

VENTER DROPS A BOMBSHELL

Venter picked up Hunkapiller's idea and ran with it. In May 1998, he announced he was starting a new company. It would use whole genome shotgun sequencing to decode the human genome. Venter named his company Celera Genomics. He borrowed *Celera* from the Latin word *celeris*, which means "swift." Celera adopted a catchy motto: "Speed matters— discovery can't wait."

Celera planned to sequence the entire human genome by 2001, at a cost of only a few hundred million dollars. This was in marked contrast to HGP's slow, costly effort. Celera would make money by selling data to biotechnology and pharmaceutical companies as the data was generated. Every three months, Celera would post its accumulated data for free on its website.

News articles portrayed Celera and the HGP as opponents in a race. They even suggested that Celera might replace the HGP altogether. Venter himself felt that having two groups working on the same project made no sense. Since Celera would be faster, Venter suggested that HGP sequence a mouse genome instead.

"We're not in the business of patenting humanity but rather of patenting genetic drugs to give human beings longer, fuller lives."

William Haseltine, biophysicist and HGS leader, 2000

BREAKING THE RULES

But HGP members did not believe Celera would actually give its data away for free. They knew that Celera could profit handsomely by keeping some—or all—of its data private. Furthermore, by taking on the sequencing of the human genome, Venter was breaking the unwritten rules of research and angering many scientists. Under these rules, it is highly unprofessional to take up another person or organization's project. Venter's mean-spirited suggestion that the HGP sequence the genome of a rodent was especially inflammatory. The HGP was funded to sequence the *human* genome. *New York Times* reporter Nicholas Wade explained, "It may not be immediately clear to members of [the U.S.] Congress [which was paying for much of the HGP] that having forfeited the grand prize of human-genome sequence, they should now be equally happy with the glory of paying for similar research on mice."

> "While establishing a monopoly on commercial uses of the human genome sequence may be in Celera's business interest, it is not in the best interests of science or the general public."
>
> Francis Collins, 2000

The HGP was in a bad position. It had invested much time, money, and effort already. It could not afford—financially or politically—to be trumped by Celera.

In June 1998, a congressional committee met to discuss the future of U.S. funding for the HGP. Venter testified that he could complete the project faster and cheaper than the HGP. He assured Congress that Celera would freely release all its sequence data four times per year. HGP scientists, in turn, argued that Celera would sacrifice accuracy for speed. And they disputed Venter's data release promises. They pointed out that Celera could not make money without withholding data.

Congress decided to continue funding the HGP. The Wellcome Trust, in turn, increased funding for the Sanger Centre. And HGP leader Francis Collins announced a new strategy. The HGP would produce a "rough draft" of the genome by 2001 and a finished sequence by 2003. The HGP would prioritize gene-rich sections of DNA, to help medical researchers develop gene therapies.

The HGP would continue to publish its data on GenBank, following the rules in the Bermuda Accord. Anyone—including Celera—could access GenBank data for free via the World Wide Web.

VENTER AND THE FRUIT FLY

Whole genome shotgun sequencing had worked beautifully for small, simple genomes. But HGP members did not believe that the technique could work on a bigger, more complex genome. Venter set out to prove them wrong.

The fruit fly has been heavily studied by geneticists ever since Morgan and his students' gene linkage studies. So the fruit fly was one of the several nonhuman genomes included in the HGP's work. Gerald Rubin, a researcher at the University of California, led the HGP's effort to sequence the fruit fly genome. Venter asked Rubin to collaborate with him in shotgun sequencing the fruit fly. Venter said he would sequence the genome ten times faster than Sulston and Waterston had sequenced the roundworm genome. HGP members were surprised and angered when Rubin agreed to work with Venter.

Venter and Rubin's team sheared the fruit fly genome into more than 1.5 million pieces and sequenced them. Celera hired computer scientist Eugene Myers to develop complex computer programs to reassemble the pieces. Myers used the map and data from clone-based sequencing that Rubin's team had already acquired as well as the data from shotgun sequencing for the reassembly. By comparing newly generated sequences with those that had been completed earlier, they saw a reasonably high degree of accuracy (less than one error per ten thousand bases). Gaps remained in the sequence, but it was complete enough for genes to be located and studied. And the method was fast. It took just four months.

TRYING TO COLLABORATE

In October 1999, Celera announced that it had sequenced one billion bases of the human genome. The next month, HGP leaders announced that they too had sequenced one billion bases. Both the HGP and Celera began to see that the competition was detrimental. The groups were duplicating each other's work, and both were hurrying too quickly. Collaboration would yield more accurate results in less time.

Representatives from the HGP and Celera met in December to work out a plan. But they could not agree on how to work together. The biggest disagreement concerned data access. Celera wanted exclusive rights to the data generated by both teams for up to five years. Collins was only willing to grant Celera rights for six months to one year.

Another source of contention was that Celera could access the HGP's data, while the HGP could not access Celera's data. Celera argued that as a taxpaying corporation, it deserved access to publicly funded data. The HGP agreed—but wanted Celera to release its data too.

Meanwhile, on January 10, 2000, Venter announced that Celera had sequenced 90 percent of the human genome.

IRRECONCILABLE DIFFERENCES

Collins kept trying to forge a collaboration. He contacted Venter many times after the December 1999 meeting—but without success. By the end of February, Collins was ready to give up. He faxed Celera a letter asking for a final response within a week.

The day before the deadline, someone leaked the letter to the press. This sparked a series of public arguments. Celera accused the HGP of sabotaging a possible collaboration through public pressure. The HGP denied this charge.

A few days later, Celera wrote the HGP expressing interest in collaborating, as long as Celera's business interests were protected. Celera repeated its promise to release its data to researchers at no cost.

On March 9, 2000, the HGP deposited the two billionth base letter of the human genome into GenBank. It had taken a mere four months to sequence

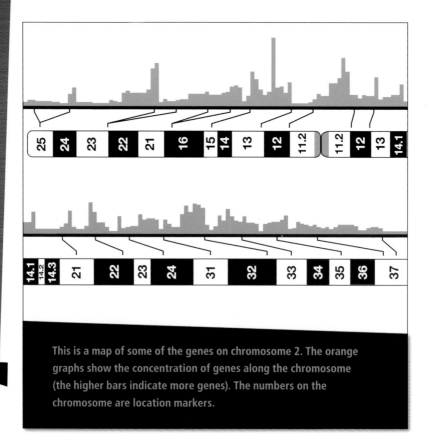

This is a map of some of the genes on chromosome 2. The orange graphs show the concentration of genes along the chromosome (the higher bars indicate more genes). The numbers on the chromosome are location markers.

the second billion bases. The HGP had picked up its pace dramatically.

On April 6, Celera announced that it had finished sequencing an entire human genome. The genome was in about thirty million fragments. Celera still needed to assemble the fragments into a complete genome. With this news, the decadelong race was finally nearing its close.

A TRUCE OVER BEER AND PIZZA

But Celera and the HGP were still bickering. As the end of the race drew near, the public dispute between the two teams got ugly. They continued to debate public access to genome data. They argued bitterly over which team deserved credit for sequencing the human genome. And each side criticized the quality of the other's genome sequence. Constant bad-mouthing between the HGP and Celera threatened the dignity of their joint accomplishment.

SIR JOHN
SULSTON

The U.S. press portrayed the human genome race as a rivalry between Venter and Collins. But in the United Kingdom, the opponents were Venter and Sulston.

The British press contrasted Venter's ostentatious lifestyle—he owned a huge yacht and a private jet—to Sulston's modest one—he drove a secondhand car. It called Venter arrogant, while portraying Sulston as modest.

Sir John Sulston poses for a photograph at the Sanger Centre in 2002.

Sulston believed that the community, not an individual or company, should control resources. He deeply opposed patenting human genetic information. He said, "I believe . . . our 'software' should be free and open for everyone to play with, to compete with, to try and make products from." This directly contrasted with Venter's belief, which said that profit from scientific research was perfectly acceptable.

President Clinton was anxious to end the bitter public dispute. Aristides Patrinos, who led the Department of Energy's share of the HGP, invited Venter and Collins to his house for beer and pizza on May 7. Over the course of several such meetings, they agreed to announce their drafts and publish their work at the same time—thus declaring the race a tie. They could not collaborate, but at least they would cooperate.

They scheduled a joint announcement for late June 2000. That left just a few weeks to finish assembling the complete genome.

THE ANNOUNCEMENT

On June 26, 2000, a satellite link between the White House and 10 Downing Street in London (the UK prime minister's residence) brought Collins, Venter, President Clinton, Sulston, and Prime Minister Tony Blair together before a global audience. As they announced the completion of the sequencing of the

On June 26, 2000, U.S. president Bill Clinton *(center)*, Francis Collins *(right)*, and Craig Venter *(left)* gathered at the White House to announce the completion of the sequencing of the human genome. Joining them by video conference were John Sulston and British prime minister Tony Blair, who spoke from London, England.

human genome, scientists and reporters around the world compared it to other monumental achievements in scientific history, such as landing humans on the moon for the first time in 1969. In spite of the hard feelings between Collins and Venter, each praised the other's contributions. Collins described Venter's technique as elegant and innovative. And he described Venter himself as articulate and provocative. Venter, in turn, complimented Collins and the HGP for their contribution to the working draft of the human genome. And he thanked Collins for working with him to develop cooperation in the genome community.

CHAPTER 6

THE FINAL ROUND

The truce didn't last. After the big announcement of the completion of the human genome project, Celera and the HGP had to publish their findings in a scientific journal.

When scientists publish their findings, they're supposed to present their supporting data so their peers can see and analyze it. Having an article published in an academic journal is an honor, so usually journal editors can insist that scientists provide all their data. But this situation was different. Publishing the HGP's or Celera's findings would bring prestige to the journal, so the rules about data were more flexible. This caused yet another conflict.

Collins and Venter had planned to publish their reports in the same issue of the same journal—either *Science* or *Nature*. The journals competed for the reports, trying to offer both teams the best terms. *Science*'s policy said data must be "deposited with the appropriate data bank." *Nature*'s policy was more explicit. It said data must be deposited in GenBank "or a database of equivalent unrestricted accessibility."

At first both groups planned to publish in *Science*. HGP members insisted on data release to GenBank as a requirement for publication. But Celera and the HGP were in different situations. Celera had spent hundreds of millions of shareholder dollars for research. According to shareholder terms, Celera was not allowed to release its data without restrictions. *Science* editor Donald Kennedy said requiring Celera to release its data to GenBank would be the same as rejecting Celera's report. *Science* and Celera reached a compromise in which Celera would release data on its own website. Users would have to register. Celera would release data free and unrestricted to academics. But it would restrict data and charge a fee to commercial users, such as biotech companies.

HGP members were incensed. They said that *Science*'s terms were discriminatory because the journal did not insist that Celera make its data freely available to all. Several HGP members wrote to Kennedy, charging *Science* with setting a bad example by letting Celera publish without providing data. Other scientists might try to do the same in the future. Geneticist Michael

"You have lowered a proud journal to the level of a newspaper Sunday supplement, accepting paid advertisement in the guise of a scientific paper.... They [Celera] want the commercial advantage of having done a whole genome shotgun sequence and they (or at least Craig) want the academic kudos which goes with it."

Michael Ashburner, British geneticist, in a letter to *Science*, 2005

Ashburner, a former *Science* editor, wrote an open letter to *Science* editors criticizing their agreement with Celera. He urged them to resign. Kennedy responded that other published scientific articles had required readers to get supporting data from independent websites. And some of those websites gave free access only to nonprofit scientists. The next day, HGP leaders voted to submit their report to *Nature* instead of *Science*. *Nature* and *Science* agreed to publish the two reports at the same time.

THE AFTERMATH

Even after the articles were published, bitter battles continued. Celera and the HGP argued over which sequence was more complete and accurate. And the HGP accused Celera of making a false claim in suggesting that it had produced its sequence using the whole genome shotgun sequencing technique. But Celera had used HGP data to produce part of the sequence. Some HGP scientists performed simulations that, they said, proved Celera couldn't have used only the whole genome shotgun method. Celera, in turn, claimed that the HGP's simulations were flawed.

Another scandal swirled around the DNA on which the genome projects were based. For ease of carrying out the projects, both the HGP and Celera produced a genome dominated by one person's DNA. The HGP took great pains to ensure that the owner of the dominant DNA in the HGP genome was anonymous and untraceable. No one—including the donors and the scientists—knew whose DNA was sequenced.

Celera claimed to have a similar—though not identical—process, with a protocol to protect the privacy of DNA donors. But after Venter left Celera in 2002, he told a reporter that his DNA dominated Celera's genome. In his autobiography, he described how he had secretly supplied DNA samples. He said he did this because following the approved protocol would have slowed Celera's progress. Celera's chief medical officer knew about Venter's donation and made sure that his samples were allowed.

Many people, including Celera's bioethics board, chastised Venter for his donation and his revelation. An editor at *Science* denounced Venter's actions as "tacky." And many people complained that Venter had violated his relatives' privacy by revealing his secret.

REPERCUSSIONS OF RIVALRY

In the end, different strategies brought Celera and the HGP similar results. Had the groups collaborated, they could have pooled their resources and saved a lot of effort, time, and money. But instead, they competed. This competition both pushed and limited each team in important ways.

Celera's key strengths were low cost and high speed. Celera spent $300 million, while the HGP spent $3 billion. And Celera's whole genome shotgun method was clearly faster than the HGP's clone-based sequencing method.

But the HGP was at it much longer. Its cost and time were not all for sequencing the human genome. It invested in improving technology and sequencing the genomes of model organisms. By the time Celera appeared, genome understanding and sequencing technology had improved dramatically, and the team benefited from the earlier work of the HGP. Also, Celera used HGP's gene maps to aid reassembly. This saved Celera both time and money. On the flip side,

"If it is the opinion of some editors that it was 'tacky,' to reveal that I was part of the sequencing pool, so be it. Opinions are like genomes: Everyone has one. I want to show the world that we do not need to fear our genetic information but, rather, that it can be a powerful new tool to help us prevent or better treat disease and lead healthier lives."

Craig Venter, 2003

scientists generally agree that Celera's pace forced the HGP to work faster. Improvements in technology would have sped up the HGP's progress anyway. But Celera's challenge provided strong financial and moral motivation to work as fast as possible. The HGP's increased speed meant that specific genes were located earlier. Medical researchers could use these genes earlier to develop tests and treatments for genetic diseases.

But the competition had drawbacks too. To speed up sequencing, the HGP received

"Without Celera's challenge, the [HGP] would have had little reason to alter its academic flight path and produce the useful part of the genome three years ahead of the 2003 landing date. Without the [HGP's] challenge, Celera could be commanding top dollar for its database, knowing customers had no alternative."

Nicholas Wade, *New York Times* reporter, 2000

Collins *(left)* and Sulston speak at an event in 2010 marking the ten-year anniversary of the first draft of the human genome.

SEQUENCING
INTO THE FUTURE

Both the HGP and Celera used the sequencing method developed by Fred Sanger in the 1970s. But modern scientists have been developing faster methods. One is called pyrosequencing. This process uses a single strand of DNA as a template. It locates all bases of the same type on that strand at once. (For example, it locates all the Cs simultaneously.) Then it locates all the bases of another type, such as A. Pyrosequencing works only for short strands of DNA.

more funding than it would have otherwise. These resources could have gone to other important programs. Another drawback was the distortion of the HGP's goal. The general public thought that the June 2000 announcement signaled the end of the race. Many people didn't realize that scientists still had years of work ahead to produce a complete, accurate human genome sequence and to locate and analyze many genes in the sequence. Finally, what should have been a calm, respectful scientific dialog became a bitter public argument. Human egos led to tension, rivalry, and scandal.

Yet, as with other scientific rivalries, the competition also led to key discoveries. Future generations of researchers will build on these discoveries to improve their understanding of human genetics.

TIMELINE

1866 Gregor Mendel carries out studies demonstrating that units causing different traits pass from parent to offspring and occur in pairs.

1910 Thomas Hunt Morgan shows that chromosomes contain genes, the carriers of hereditary information.

1944 Oswald Avery and his colleagues demonstrate that DNA carries genetic information.

1953 James Watson and Francis Crick discover the structure of DNA, based on key work by Rosalind Franklin.

1958 Francis Crick describes how DNA directs protein synthesis.

1970 Hamilton Smith finds the first restriction enzyme that cuts at a specific site in DNA.

1977 Frederick Sanger and his colleagues report the first sequence of a complete genome.

1986 Renato Dulbecco proposes the sequencing of the human genome.

1989 Scientists locate the gene encoding cystic fibrosis on the human genome.

1990 The Human Genome Project (HGP) officially begins.

1992 Francis Collins replaces James Watson as the leader of the U.S. arm of the HGP. Craig Venter leaves the National Institutes of Health (NIH) for The Institute for Genomic Research (TIGR).

1993 Harold Varmus replaces Bernadine Healy as NIH director.

1995 Smith and Venter sequence the genomes of *Haemophilus influenzae* and *Mycoplasma genitalium* using the whole genome shotgun technique.

1996 HGP leaders develop the Bermuda Accord to promote data sharing. The HGP completes the yeast genome sequence.

1998 Venter announces his intention to sequence the human genome. HGP scientists sequence the first full genome of an animal.

1999 Venter and Gerald Rubin sequence the fruit fly genome using whole genome shotgun sequencing.

2000 Venter, Collins, and John Sulston jointly announce the completed sequence of the human genome.

2010 Venter creates the first synthetic life-form by building a genome and incorporating it into a cell.

2012 Researchers in Cambridge sequence the gorilla genome, enabling scientists to compare the human genome to that of all types of apes. (Chimpanzee and orangutan genomes had already been sequenced.)

GLOSSARY

bacterial artificial chromosome (BAC): in human genome sequencing, an artificial chromosome composed of both bacterial and human DNA. HGP scientists used BACs for cloning and sequencing DNA.

base: a basic component of DNA. The bases that occur in DNA are adenine (A), thymine (T), guanine (G), and cytosine (C).

chromosome: a long, coiled strand of DNA found in the cells of living things

expressed sequence tags (ESTs): DNA made using mRNA as a template. ESTs represent genes rather than noncoding DNA.

GenBank: a publicly available database of DNA sequences and their protein translations

genome: all the genetic information in an organism

noncoding DNA: DNA that is not transcribed to mRNA. Noncoding DNA is sometimes called junk DNA.

patent: an exclusive right granted by the government that allows an inventor to make, use, or sell an invention for a limited period of time

restriction enzyme: protein that cuts DNA at a specific sequence of bases

sequencing: determining the order of bases in DNA or RNA

whole genome shotgun sequencing: a method of sequencing in which a whole genome is randomly broken into fragments

SOURCE NOTES

5 Leslie Roberts, "Controversial from the Start," *Science*, February 16, 2001, http://cmbi.bjmu.edu.cn/news/0102/36.htm (September 15, 2011).

7 J. Craig Venter, *A Life Decoded: My Genome: My Life* (New York: Penguin Group, 2007), 298.

10 Ian Shine and Sylvia Wrobel, *Thomas Hunt Morgan: Pioneer of Genetics* (Lexington: University Press of Kentucky, 1976), 92.

12 Max Perutz, "Co-chairman's Remarks: Before the Double Helix," *Gene*, December 1993, 12.

19 Renato Dulbecco, "A Turning Point in Cancer Research: Sequencing the Human Genome," *Science*, March 1986, 1,056.

21 Nicholas Wade, "Reading the Book of Life: A Historic Quest; Double Landmarks for Watson: Helix and Genome," *New York Times*, June 27, 2000, http://www.nytimes.com/2000/06/27/science/reading-book-life-historic-quest-double-landmarks-for-watson-helix-genome.html?pagewanted=all&src=pm (November 9, 2011).

21 Ibid.

22 International Human Genome Sequencing Consortium, "Initial Sequencing and Analysis of the Human Genome," *Nature*, January 9, 2001, http://www.nature.com/nature/journal/v409/n6822/full/409860a0.html (November 9, 2011).

25 Douglas Birch, "Daring Sprint to the Summit," *Baltimore Sun*, April 13, 1999.

27 Venter, *A Life Decoded*, 111.

27 Robert Cooke-Deegan, *The Gene Wars: Science, Politics, and the Human Genome* (New York: W. W. Norton, 1994), 315.

29 Peter Aldhous, "MRC Follows NIH on Patents," *Nature*, March 12, 1992, 98.

29 American Association for the Advancement of Science, "Genome Patent Fight Erupts,"

Science, October 11, 1991, http://www.sciencemag.org/content/254/5029/184.extract (November 14, 2011).

30 Kevin Davies, *Cracking the Genome: Inside the Race to Unlock Human DNA* (Baltimore: Johns Hopkins University Press, 2001), 63.

30 Leslie Roberts, "Why Watson Quit as Project Head," *Science*, April 17, 1992, 302.

35 Davies, *Cracking the Genome*, 63.

37 John Maddox, "Directory to the Human Genome," *Nature*, August 10, 1995, 459–460.

39 Davies, *Cracking the Genome*, 87.

41 Ibid., 93.

42 Venter, *A Life Decoded*, 234.

42 British Broadcasting Corporation, "Genome Pioneer Steps Down," *BBC News*, January 22, 2002, http://news.bbc.co.uk/2/hi/science/nature/1775289.stm (November 28, 2011).

42 William Haseltine, "21st Century Genes," *Washington Post*, March 28, 2000.

43 Davies, *Cracking the Genome*, 204.

43 Ibid., 150.

47 K. Perry, "The Key Players," *Guardian* (London), June 26, 2000.

51 Declan Butler, "US/UK Statement on Genome Data Prompts Debate on 'Free Access,'" *Nature*, March 21, 2000, 325.

51 Ibid.

51 James Shreeve, *The Genome War: How Craig Venter Tried to Capture the Code of Life and Save the World* (New York: Ballantine, 2005), 361.

53 Donald Kennedy, "Not Wicked Perhaps, but Tacky," *Science*, August 23, 2002, 1,237.

53 Craig Venter, "A Part of the Human Genome Sequence, *Science*, February 21, 2003, 1,184.

54 Shreeve, *The Genome War*, 361.

SELECTED BIBLIOGRAPHY

Collins, Francis, Ari Patrinos, Elke Jordan, Aravinda Chakravarti, Raymond Gesteland, LeRoy Walters, Eric Fearon, et al. "New Goals for the U.S. Human Genome Project: 1998–2003." *Science*, October 23, 1998, 682–689.

Cooke-Deegan, Robert. *The Gene Wars: Science, Politics, and the Human Genome*. New York: W. W. Norton, 1994.

Davies, Kevin. *Cracking the Genome: Inside the Race to Unlock Human DNA*. Baltimore: Johns Hopkins University Press, 2001.

Eisenberg, R. S., and R. R. Nelson. "Public vs. Proprietary Science: A Fruitful Tension?" *Academic Medicine*, December 2002, 1,392–1,399.

Lander, E. S., L. M. Linton, B. Birren, C. Nusbaum, M. C. Zody, J. Baldwin, K. Devon, et al. "Initial Sequencing and Analysis of the Human Genome." *Nature*, February 15, 2001, 860–921.

Marshall, Eliot. "Sharing the Glory, Not the Credit." *Science*, February 16, 2001, 1,189–1,193.

————. "Storm Erupts over Terms for Publishing Celera's Sequence." *Science*, December 15, 2000, 2,042–2,043.

Olson, Maynard. "The Human Genome Project: A Player's Perspective." *Journal of Molecular Biology*, April 11, 2002, 931–942.

Roberts, Leslie. "Controversial from the Start." *Science*, February 16, 2001, 1,182–1,188.

Sanger Centre and Washington University Genome Sequencing Center. "Toward a Complete Human Genome Sequence." *Genome Research*, November 1998, 1,097–1,108.

Sulston, John. "Heritage of Humanity." *Le Monde Diplomatique*, December 2002. http://mondediplo .com/2002/12/15genome (June 2, 2010).

Venter, J. Craig. *A Life Decoded: My Genome: My Life*. New York: Penguin Group, 2007.

Venter, J. Craig, M. D. Adams, E. W. Myers, P. W. Li, R. J. Mural, G. G. Sutton, H. O. Smith, et al. "The Sequence of the Human Genome." *Science*, February 16, 2001, 1,304–1,351.

Wadman, Meredith. "Human Genome Deadline Cut by Two Years." *Nature*, September 17, 1998, 207.

Watson, James D., Richard M. Myers, Amy A. Caudy, and Jan A. Witkowski. *Recombinant DNA: Genes and Genomes—a Short Course*. 3rd ed. New York: W. H. Freeman, 2007.

FURTHER INFORMATION

BOOKS

Ballen, Karen Gunnison. *Seven Wonders of Medicine*. Minneapolis: Twenty-First Century Books, 2010. This colorful book includes seven wonders of modern medical science, including a chapter on the Human Genome Project.

Cherfas, Jeremy. *The Human Genome*. London: Dorling Kindersley, 2002. This brief book explains the history of genetics and basic information about the Human Genome Project.

Fridell, Ron. *Decoding Life: Unraveling the Mysteries of the Genome*. Minneapolis: Lerner Publications Company, 2006. Fridell explores the potential of genetic engineering as well as the ethical questions it brings.

Guttman, Burton, Anthony Griffiths, David Suzuki, and Tara Cullis. *Genetics: The Code of Life*. New York: Rosen Publishing, 2011. This book covers the history of genetics, the functions of genes, the structure of DNA, the human genome, and DNA manipulation.

Johnson, Rebecca L. *Genetics*. Minneapolis: Twenty-First Century Books, 2006. Johnson explains the history of genetics and how it relates to biotechnology.

Jones, Phill. *The Genetic Code*. New York: Chelsea House, 2010. This book reviews the key experiments and discoveries regarding the genetic code and explores the ways humans have used this knowledge to genetically modify plants and animals and to alter genes in human cells.

WEBSITES

DNA Learning Center
http://www.dnalc.org
Follow the link to "websites" for educational material on topics ranging from the basics of heredity to the influence of genes on your health.

DNA Learning Center: Sequencing Head to Toe
http://www.dnalc.org/view/15910-Sequencing-head-to-toe.html
This site at the DNA Learning Center features an interactive diagram that explains the complex process of cloned-based sequencing step-by-step.

DNA Workshop
http://www.pbs.org/wgbh/aso/tryit/dna/#
This website puts you inside a cell to see how DNA replication and protein synthesis work.

Genetic Science Learning Center
http://learn.genetics.utah.edu
The University of Utah provides this interactive website. It features basic information on DNA structure and the transcription and translation of genes as well as issues in biotechnology.

Human Genome Project Information
http://www.ornl.gov/sci/techresources/Human_Genome/home.shtml
This website from the U.S. Department of Energy is a rich source of information about many different aspects of the Human Genome Project.

J. Craig Venter Institute
http://www.jcvi.org
This website explains the many programs run by the institute established by Craig Venter after he left Celera.

"Last of the Neanderthals"
http://ngm.nationalgeographic.com/2008/10/neanderthals/hall-text/1
This *National Geographic* article explains how scientists used a combination of different data—including genetic analyses—to determine how Neanderthals lived and what they looked like.

Microbial Genomics at the U.S. Department of Energy
http://microbialgenomics.energy.gov/index.shtml
Follow the link called "Educational Tools" to find information about microorganisms and the importance of studying microbial genomes.

"Online Education Kit: Understanding the Human Genome Project"
http://www.genome.gov/25019879
This website from the National Institutes of Health includes videos showing the importance of genetics in human history, how to sequence a gene, and the legal and ethical implications of genetic knowledge.

Synthetic Genomics
http://www.syntheticgenomics.com
Synthetic Genomics is a company cofounded by Craig Venter. The company uses genetically modified microorganisms to produce biofuels.

Your Genes, Your Health
http://www.yourgenesyourhealth.org
This website from Cold Spring Harbor Laboratory explains the causes, symptoms, and treatments for a number of genetic disorders.

INDEX

PHOTO ACKNOWLEDGMENTS

The images in this book are used with the permission of: AP Photo/Ruth Fremson, p. 5 (left); Courtesy of National Human Genome Research Institute or NHGRI, p. 5 (right); © Laura Weslund/Independent Picture Service, pp. 6, 15; © Hutlon Archive/Stringer/Getty Images, p. 9 (top); © Biophoto Associates/Photo Researchers, Inc., p. 9 (bottom); © Omikron/Photo Researchers, Inc., p. 12; © National Library of Medicine/Photo Researchers, Inc., p. 13; © A. Barrington Brown/Photo Researchers, Inc., p. 14; Courtesy of the Archives, California Institute of Technology, p. 19; Wellcome Library, London, p. 22; Gerald Baber, Virginia Tech/National Science Foundation, p. 24 (all); Tim Shaffer/RTR/Information Partner/Newscom, p. 41; © Bill Hauser/National Center for Biotechnology Information, p. 46; © Scott Barbour/Stringer/Getty Images, p. 47; Ron Sachs- CNP/Newscom, p. 48; © Copyright Guardian News & Media Ltd 2010, p. 54.

Front cover: © Can Stock Photo Inc./Eraxion.

Main body text set in Frutiger LT Std 11/15. Typeface provided by Adobe Systems.

ABOUT THE AUTHOR

Karen Gunnison Ballen has a bachelor's degree from Kalamazoo College in Michigan and a doctoral degree from the University of Minnesota. She teaches at the University of Minnesota and writes books and magazine articles for young people about nature and medicine. *Decoding Our DNA* is her third book.